T0055863

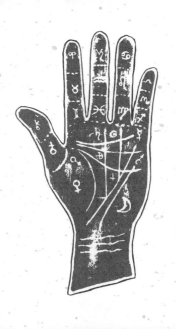

The Art of

PALMiSTRY

—⋈ △ ⋈—

Vernon Mahabal

MANDALA

CONTENTS

WHAT iS
PALMISTRY?

Your hands contain information that
explain your true talents and abilities.
They express what you are good at
doing and what will make you happy.
Your hands explain these things in
symbols, like a secret code. To learn
how to read palms is to unlock this
secret code. Very few people in this
world know how to do this, but many
great kings, queens, magicians, and
conquerors of the ancient world knew
how to read hands. Being a palmist is
like being a detective. When you are
looking at palms, you are like a private

investigator who sees clues and figures out what they mean.

Think of the hand as a road map of your life. Just as geographical maps are helpful when you're walking around an unfamiliar city or visiting a foreign country, the maps on your palms can help you navigate life. Like paper maps, they let us know where we are, what we will be able to see and do, and the fastest ways to get around. The maps on our hands also let us know our own individual talents and abilities, so if we learn to read our maps, we'll know where to focus our efforts, and life will become easier for us. When we understand what we are naturally good at, it will be easier to become strong and confident.

Some people may tell you that palmistry is supernatural, occult, or even creepy. Only those who have no real knowledge about palmistry will say these things. There is nothing to be afraid of with palmistry. Hand reading is a science, just like the science of medicine or technology. Many of the great ancient civilizations believed in palmistry. Other people will ask you, "What if my hand says something bad?" When they do, you can tell them that palmistry explains what you are good at doing, and what will make you happy. If you have difficulties in life, the hands will always show how to work through them.

Learning to read hands is enjoyable, and it's something that can really help people. As you read more and more hands, you'll want to learn as much as you can about palmistry. Carry this book around with you and look up information as you need. After you've understood everything in this book, you might want to read other books on palmistry to learn more. You can also learn by talking to, or even studying with, other palmists. Palmistry is a fascinating science!

How I Became a Palmist

— — ᗯᗯᑎ ᘓ ᗯᗯᗯ — —

My introduction to palmistry began
when I bought a book about it that was
written over one hundred years ago. It
taught a very ancient form of palmistry,
and reading it took me into the world
of palmistry's rich history. Most of
its ideas were very outdated, but I had
enough information to get started.

A couple of years later, I met a palmist named Patrick who read hands at a
table on St. Mark's Place in New York
City. Listening to him give readings
made me want to learn palmistry
myself, so I read every book on the
topic that I could find, and looked at
many different hands. Sometimes, I
rode the subway and gave people readings on their way to work. I also deeply

enjoyed meeting other palmists and sharing information with them. That is how my palmistry career began.

Since then, I've read thousands of hands and given hundreds of classes. As a palmist, I've met fascinating people and traveled to many interesting places.

You can read this book to unlock the secrets of your own hands, or the hands of others, as I have done. Whichever you desire, the path of palmistry is very powerful. The more that you look at other people's hands, the more you learn about yourself. You will never get bored with palmistry.

Every person is an individual—and therefore every hand is completely different. You will see or learn something new every time you study a hand. When you look into a person's palm, you are looking at the gateway to their soul.

How to Give a
Palmistry Reading

—— ⁓⁓⁓ ☽ ⌄⌄⌄ ——

You and your querent—the person who
is getting a reading from you—should
sit across from each other.

You should both be very comfortable
and relaxed.

Ask the querent if they are right-
handed or left-handed. Look at both
hands, but most of your attention
should be on their main hand. The
main hand is the right hand for
right-handers, and the left hand for
left-handers.

To read a hand properly, you need
enough light to see it clearly. You can
read a hand in the sunlight, or you can
use a table lamp.

It is always better to read the querent's hand in a quiet and private area. Do palmistry in a place where you will not be disturbed.

A palmist always keeps their readings confidential. Never tell others what you have seen on a person's hand, even if their friends ask you! A reading is only between you and the querent. It is private.

If you start to read hands regularly, buy a small magnifying glass. An experienced palmist is never without their magnifying glass.

Tell your querent only what you see on their hands. Never make anything up! Remember that people never forget the words of a palmist—so be truthful.

The last and most important rule in palmistry: Read hands to help people. Never do it to show off!

PART I:
HANDS

⚔ △ ⚔

Which Hand Do You Read?

— — ⋙ ☾ ⋘ — —

As you are learning to be a palmist, you may wonder which hand to look at. Do you read both hands, or just one? If you are only going to look at someone's palms for a few minutes, ask them which hand they write with and read that one.

If you have more time to look at your friend's hands, then you should read both and compare them with each other, but the most important hand to focus on will still be their main hand. Palmists call the hand that you write with or eat with your main hand. For most people, the main hand will be the right one. Most people are right-handed, and it's a lot easier to be that way in our world, because most things are made for right-hand use.

What if you or your friend is left-handed? Did you know that if you put one hundred people in a room, about fifteen of them will be left-handed? To be left-handed is very special. You should be proud if you are a lefty. As a left-hander, you have a very strong inner voice. This means that you can listen to your heart or feelings and hear the right answers. Right-handers may also have this voice, of course, but they tend to ignore it because they don't trust it. Righties feel more comfortable when they make choices using their mind and intelligence, and left-handed people are happier following their hearts. A lefty will usually want to do things differently—which is part of the reason that many great artists and musicians throughout history have been left-handed. They did things in unique ways, and that helped lead to their successes.

Hand Colors
–– ∿∿ ☾ ∿∿ ––

The color of your palms can sometimes change. Most of the time, your palms will be a shade of pink, but now and then, your palms will change to a different color. Keep your eyes open for this. The different colors can tell you about how a person is feeling.

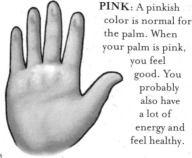

PINK: A pinkish color is normal for the palm. When your palm is pink, you feel good. You probably also have a lot of energy and feel healthy.

RED: When your palm looks reddish, it usually means that you're upset or mad at someone. Most of the time, it's because they won't let you do something that you really want to do. Watch your temper. If your hands are very red, you will feel like fighting— exercising or playing sports will help get rid of your anger.

YELLOW: When you have a yellowish palm, it means that you are worrying too much about something. Something is bothering you. And a very yellow palm means that you have been criticizing other people—calling them names or making fun of them, so try giving advice instead—especially because very yellow palms also mean you really want people to listen to you.

WHITE: When your palms look a little white, you need some time alone; you might not want to talk to anyone for a while. It might be apparent in your life, to the extent that your friends may be wondering what's wrong. If your palms are very white, you are feeling lazy—you might want to just stay in bed all day.

BLUE: Bluish palms indicate that something's on your mind, and if your palms are very blue, you are feeling very sad. Talk to someone you love or feel very close to. Get your feelings out!

Hand Shapes

—— ∿∿ ☾ ∿∿ ——

The shape of the hand is essential to note because it is a physical representation of our most basic character traits and approach to life. The four basic hand shapes correspond to the four ancient elements of earth, air, fire, and water.

EARTH (The Pragmatist): Earth Hands have square palms and somewhat short-looking fingers. People with these hands are drawn to establishing firm foundations, often seeking out security, stability, and a steady income. They are realists and like concrete results.

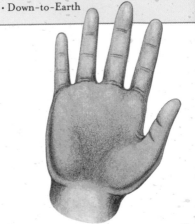

KEY IDEAS:
· Organized, Methodical, and Practical
· Resistant to Change
· Seeks Structure and Routine
· Down-to-Earth

WATER (The Receptive One): Water Hands have long palms and elongated fingers. These people are attracted to activities that involve healing, art, beauty, and creativity. They experience life through their feelings and intuition.

KEY IDEAS:
- Sensitive, Intuitive, and Gentle
- Refined, Imaginative, and Moody
- Soft-spoken, Empathetic, and Responsive
- Dreamy

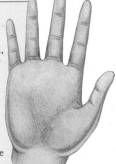

KEY IDEAS:

- Assertive, Self-Motivated, and Fiery
- Zealous and Intense
- Likes Excitement and Attention
- Shows initiative

FIRE (The Passionate One): Fire Hands have a slightly long palm combined with short-looking fingers. Fire-Handed people seek a life that is adventurous and challenging. They strive to create personal independence.

AIR (The Expressive One): Air Hands have square palms and longer-looking fingers. These people love to learn and share their ideas with others. They interpret life through logic and reason.

KEY IDEAS:

- Sociable, Inquisitive, and Studious
- Investigative and Curious
- Brainstormer and Debater
- An Ideas Person

Palm Shapes

— - ⋀⋀⋀ ☾ ⋁⋁⋁ - —

The shape of your palm is very important because it describes your basic personality. The qualities indicated by the shape of your palm form the foundations of your life, and tell you how to best take part in life.

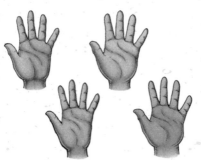

SQUARE: You like to spend a lot of time outdoors. Your body is probably strong, and you may like to play sports and be active. It's not important for you to have many friends—just a few very good ones. Also, you do not like a lot of change in your life. In fact, if you can follow a regular schedule, you'll get a lot of things done. You are also probably great at building and constructing things.

RECTANGLE: You possess a great imagination, and you probably dream a lot. Write down your ideas every day. You may also enjoy writing poetry or short stories. You are very warm to others, and you may be very emotional and sensitive at times. Your feelings are important to you. You like a lot of peace in your life, and you don't like fighting and arguing. You enjoy spending time alone. You are very loving toward those you care about. People with rectangular palms are usually very artistic.

ROUND: You like to have a lot of friends. You enjoy parties and entertainment. You love meeting new people and sharing ideas with others. You also like to help people. You love attention from others. You are very open-minded, and you might work to help others later in your life. People with round palms also get bored very easily.

TRIANGULAR: You can be a very restless person. You like to do things that are adventurous, like climbing mountains or hiking. You dislike sitting at home. You like to discover and explore all kinds of things. You are always busy and energetic. You love freedom and don't like people telling you what to do. You are also a leader, and you like to be in charge.

Hard & Soft Hands

— ∿∿ ☾ ∿∿ —

This section is all about *hands*-on experience! You'll need to read it two or three times while constantly checking the hardness or softness of at least five people's hands. I suggest that you read this section once quickly, then examine as many palms as possible. Then come back and reread it until you get a feel for the hardness and softness of hands.

The feel—the hardness or softness—of the hand shows how we interact with the world. This exercise might be difficult to try on yourself, but it's very easy to try on others. Place your fingers over the top of a person's hand and press your thumb down right in the middle of their palm. Does the hand feel hard, medium, or soft? Don't just feel the skin; squeeze down on the whole palm!

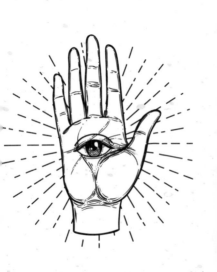

33

HARD HANDS: Hard hands feel like a hard pencil eraser.

> People with hard hands:
> · Have lots of physical energy.
> · Are always busy and active.
> · May spend a lot of time outdoors.
> · Are very determined to get what they want.
> · Can be very opinionated and closed off to other people's views.
> · Do not like doing things unless they can get something out of it.
> · Can sometimes be stubborn or pushy.

MEDIUM HANDS: Medium hands feel firm, like a ripe peach.

> **People with medium hands:**
> · Have a healthy body.
> · Get along well with others.
> · Have a positive attitude.
> · Like to work hard and
>   play hard.
> · Are very responsible.

SOFT HANDS: These hands feel like an overripe banana.

> **People with soft hands:**
> · Are easygoing and relaxed.
> · Enjoy life.
> · Like beautiful things and good-tasting foods.
> · Are very helpful, warm, and sensitive to others.
> · Like to do things indoors.

VERY SOFT HANDS: Very soft hands feel squishy, like a marshmallow. You will rarely come across very soft hands.

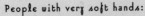

People with very soft hands:
· Tend to be low-energy.
· Seek out luxury and comfort.
· Like to be pampered.

Thick & Thin Hands

-- ∿∿ ☽ ∿∿ --

If you look at your hands from the side, you will see that they're either thick or thin. Look at other people's hands and compare them with yours.

THIN: These belong to people who spend much time in thought. They may think about philosophy, science, or spiritual topics. Most of the time, they like peace and quiet around them. They might be a bit shy.

If your hands are somewhere in between, you will have some of the qualities of both the thick-hand and the thin-hand personality types.

THICK: Found in people who are outgoing or extroverted. They love partying, meeting people, and socializing. They are bold around others and tend to be loud.

Mountains on Your Hand

–— ∧∧∧ ☾ ∨∨∨ —–

On your palm, you will find upraised pads of flesh that palmists call mountains. There are eight main mountains, and each has the qualities of one particular planet in our solar system. To be a true mountain, it must rise up like a little pillow, and it might feel soft when you press down on it. To have a mountain on your palm means that the energy of a particular planet is within you.

Some people will have only one or two mountains developed. Others, though, will have three or four mountains. Do not worry if you see that other people have more mountains than you. It may be better to have just one or two mountains, because it will be easier for you to focus your talents. If many of your mountains are developed, you will have many talents available to you, but it may be hard for you to choose which ones to pursue. People with many different mountains on their palms must consciously learn how to use all of their talents together. *This is a basic principle of palmistry: If it's large in your hand, it's large in your life.*

Compare your hand with the diagram and look at each of the nine noted areas. Each area will either be flat or have a developed mountain. The following pages will explain what each mountain means for you, if you have it.

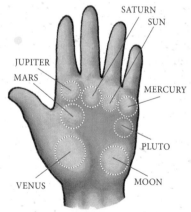

The Sun

You are an artistic person. You are very dramatic and may love to act or be a comedian. You want attention from others and enjoy being onstage.

The owner of a Sun Mountain will be very potent and impactful in the world of self-expression.

KEY IDEAS:
- Possesses a Public Persona
- Tendency Toward Personal Display
- Taste and Individuality
- In the Spotlight

The Moon

The Moon indicates a strong need for emotional connection with others. With this feature prominent, you have a very good imagination. You are definitely a dreamer. Put your ideas into something creative, like art or music.

KEY IDEAS:
- Sensitive
- Sympathetic and Warm
- Needs to Feel Wanted
- Values Communion with Others

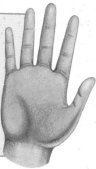

Terpsichore

△

The only nonplanetary mountain, the Dancer, can be seen as related to the Moon. This area forms a pad that can sometimes dip slightly into the wrist area. It indicates the talent of physical artistry.

KEY IDEAS:
- Possesses Physical Poise and Grace
- Involved in Dance, Drama, or Acting
- May Practice Yoga
- Theatrical

Mercury

You are very good at speaking and communicating. You are very curious, and you like to know about everything around you. You may also enjoy writing.

This pad sits directly underneath the Mercury Finger. Not only can it rise upward, but it can also slightly extend the edge of the palm. A Mercury Mountain bestows excellent mental and communicative agility, primarily in the realm of business.

KEY IDEAS:
- Good Speaking and Mediation Skills
- Understands Human Nature
- Good at Buying, Selling, and Making Deals
- Persuasive and Diplomatic

Venus

You are a very warm and friendly person. You love to go to parties and meet people. You are attracted to beautiful things like fine clothes, cars, and artwork.

The need and desire to enjoy the physical world increases with the size of this mountain.

KEY IDEAS:
- Seeks Pleasure and Sensuality
- Likes Recreation and Comfort
- Has a Keen Aesthetic Sense
- Indulgent

Mars

You are a very active person. You like to play sports and love to compete. You are also a very brave person.

An upraised Mars Mountain indicates the ability to take action.

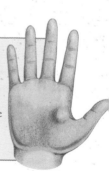

KEY IDEAS:
- Assertive and Bold
- Courageous and Energetic
- Vigorous
- A Go-Getter

Jupiter

You want to be the best at whatever you do and enjoy being a leader. You are a very confident person.

Someone who possesses this mountain sets goals and strives to achieve them.

KEY IDEAS:
· Aspiring and Confident
· Hopeful and Determined
· Strives for Growth and Abundance

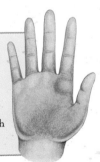

Saturn

You are a very serious person. You like to study and learn things. You love to collect knowledge and information. You may also enjoy spending time alone.

Even a slight protrusion here evidences the strength to seriously commit to duties, obligations, and responsibilities.

KEY IDEAS:
- Self-Disciplined and Focused
- Industrious
- Diligent and Hard-working
- Responsible

Pluto

You are a fighter, crusader, or warrior.
You stand up for what you believe in.
You don't believe in giving up.

KEY IDEAS:
· Fights for
  Personal Beliefs
· Political or Social
  Involvement
· Physically/
  Mentally
  Self-Disciplined
· May Practice
  Martial Arts

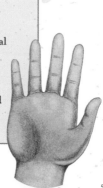

PART II:
FINGERS

✳ △ ✳

Examining the Fingers

—— ⋀⋀⋀ (⋁⋁⋁ ——

Now we will look at your fingers. It is
our fingers (and thumbs) that allow us
to do so many things with our hands.
The palms contain many types of
energies, but it is the fingers' job to
bring those energies out to the world.
Our fingers also bring in energies from
the world around us and direct them
into our palms. They thus act like trees,
which bring energies out of the Earth
and take energies in from the Sun.

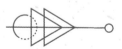

Finger Length

— — ∿∿ ☾ ∿∿ — —

To find out what those energies are—and
what energies affect us—the first thing to
look at is the finger length. Do you have
long or short fingers? If you start to look
at a lot of hands, you will quickly notice
that people have either long or short fingers. Compare the lengths of the fingers
with the palm. If the fingers look almost
as long as the palm, they are long fingers.
Fingers that look much smaller than the
length of the palm are considered short
fingers. Now look at your hands or your
friend's hands—are the fingers long, or
short? Don't get your ruler out when you
do this. Trust your eyes and your very
first thought. Your first guess will almost
always be right.

SHORT FINGERS: If you have short fingers, you don't like to sit around for too long. You like to hurry up and get things done. Short-fingered people like to take action. They are the type of people who cannot wait to play with the latest gadget. If someone is showing them how to do something, they usually can't wait to try it out. Those who have short fingers like to have many friends. They enjoy being surrounded by active and exciting people. Short-fingered people are also ambitious. If they know what their goals are, they will accomplish them. Laziness is not a quality associated with short fingers, but if you have short fingers, it may be a good idea to learn patience.

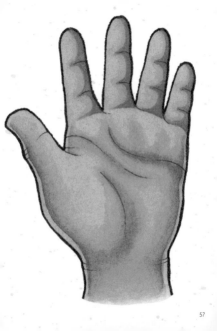

LONG FINGERS: If you have long
fingers, you are thoughtful and
like to take your time with things.
It's important to you to do things
well. You especially do not like to
be rushed. Whether you work on a
school project or on your own hobby,
you like to do things carefully and
accurately, and you have an eye for
detail. If you were to draw a tree, you
would probably add birds or draw very
detailed leaves.

Long-fingered people like to be
by themselves much of the time.
When they do socialize, they prefer
to be with one or two good friends.
People with long fingers also get their
feelings hurt easily, so if you have
long fingers, don't take others' mean
comments too seriously.

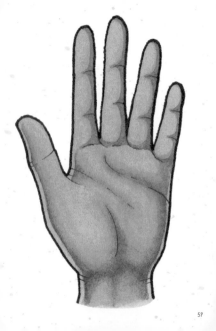

Jupiter & Sun Fingers

— ∿∿ ☾ ∿∿ —

The fingers are named after the planets because they hold the energies of the planets within them. The longer fingers are considered stronger than the others. This means that the energies of some planets are more active within you than others. This is particularly true of Jupiter and the Sun.

Start your exploration of the fingers by comparing the length of your finger of Jupiter with that of your finger of the Sun. Place your hand palm down on a desk or table. Hold your fingers close together so that there are no spaces between them. Look at both your Jupiter Finger and Sun Finger. Which is longer?

The finger of Jupiter contains the energies of power and leadership.

The finger of the Sun contains the energies of creativity and individuality.

Sometimes both fingers seem equally long. If this is true for you, pick the finger that looks wider and fatter. That will be your stronger finger. In the pages that follow, we'll delve deeper into what these differences mean.

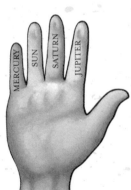

MERCURY SUN SATURN JUPITER

LONGER JUPITER: If your finger of Jupiter is longer than your Sun Finger, you have natural leadership abilities. Organizing people and giving direction to others is your greatest talent. Because you always like to be the boss, you may not like it when others tell you what to do. Many great military generals and presidents of companies have longer Jupiter Fingers. People who have longer Jupiter Fingers also like to help others. They like to do things that make life better for others, such as donating money or volunteering for charities. Those tendencies are more pronounced as you get older.

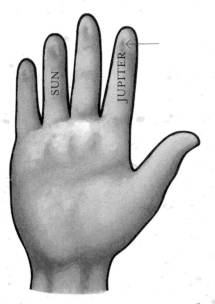

SUN

JUPITER

LONGER SUN: If your Sun Finger is longer than your Jupiter Finger, doing artistic or creative things is very important to you. Many famous musicians and artists have longer Sun Fingers. Having creative hobbies—playing music, drawing, building things—makes you happy. You also like to be popular, and become bored when people do not give you enough attention. Standing out in a crowd and being different from others are more important to you than being in charge.

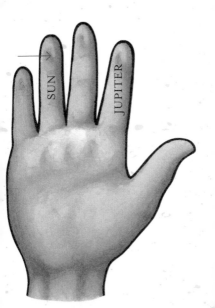

SUN

JUPITER

Jupiter Fingertips

— — ∿∿∿ ☾ ∿∿∿ — —

Jupiter is the planet of spirituality,
faith, beliefs, and hopes. The shape of
the upper tip portion of the Jupiter
Finger indicates the specific type of
spirituality that one is attracted to.
There are four fingertip shapes that
will be broken down across the next few
pages: Earth, Water, Fire, and Air.

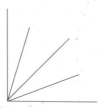

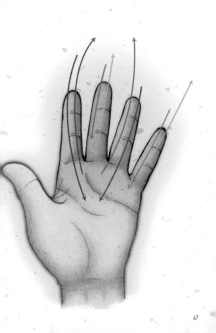

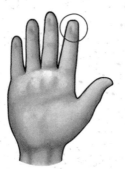

EARTH: The Earth Fingertip is flat on top. Found on the Jupiter Finger, this means that you enjoy being part of an organized spiritual group or movement. You are very attracted to religious ceremonies, rituals, and traditions. You are also inspired by large temples, cathedrals, and beautiful churches.

WATER: The Water Fingertip is pointed, and having it means that the world of prophecy, intuition, and psychic energy very much interests you. You have a strong inner faith in everything spiritual, and do not require proof for your beliefs. Above all, you are attracted to the devotional pastimes of love and friendship between God/Goddess and their devotees.

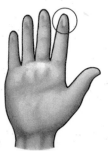

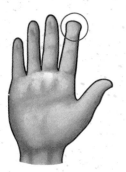

FIRE: The Fire Fingertip looks like a small spatula. If your Jupiter fingertip has this shape, you have very individualistic and unique spiritual views. People who create new religious or spiritual movements possess this finger shape. You may one day become a spiritual warrior or crusader.

AIR: The Air Fingertip is rounded. If your Jupiter Finger has this tip, then you consider the most important part of a spiritual path to be the philosophy behind it. The things you enjoy most are reading scriptures, collecting knowledge, and discovering ancient wisdom. People with this fingertip like to see connections, rather than differences, between science and religion.

Finger Spacing

—— 〰〰 ☾ 〰〰 ——

There are eight Great Elements. They
are Earth, Water, Fire, Air, Ether,
Mind, Intelligence, and Ego. Four of
these are physical, three are subtle,
and one both. The physical elements
are Earth, Water, Fire, and Air. These
physical elements can be experienced
through touch, sight, hearing, taste,
and smell. The subtle elements are
Mind, Intelligence, and Ego. They
cannot be perceived by our senses
because they represent our spirit
consciousness, or soul. The element
of Ether is on the borderline between
being physical and subtle. Sound
vibration is actually a product of the
Etheric world. Sound is carried by
Air, but it is not produced by Air, but
by the Ether. Everything physically

produced in this world begins from sound vibration.

For example, after a plan is conceived by the mind and intelligence, it is carried out into practical reality by the use of speech, words, and discussions. In this way, the element of Ether forms the bridge between consciousness and matter.

This invisible element of Ether surrounds our hands. Place your hands on a table and relax them. Are there spaces between your fingers, or do some of the fingers stay closer together? If there are spaces, it means that the Ether is flowing freely around the hand. This is a sign of a strong connection between the mind and the body, which grants the ability to easily carry out plans. Any clinging together of the fingers, or thumb to the palm, shows that Ether is blocked from that space, limiting its power.

SPACES: If there are spaces between all of your fingers and your thumb, this is a positive indication that your talents are manifesting. Also, the wider the spaces, the more confident and independent you'll be.

CLINGING: If all of your fingers cling closely together, you are definitely holding back your abilities. You are also shy and reserved.

Between the Thumb
and the Hand

SPACE: You have the ability to shape and control situations around you.

CLINGING: When the thumb clings to the hand, you find it hard to influence and control things around you, and you may have little interest in doing so.

———

Between the Jupiter
and Saturn Fingers

SPACE: It's easy for you to act independently and do things on your own.

CLINGING: You may be dependent on others and wait for them to take the lead.

Between the Mercury and Sun Fingers

SPACE: You have the desire and ability to communicate your ideas and opinions.

CLINGING: You may be hesitant or reluctant to communicate your thoughts and ideas.

Between the Saturn and Sun Fingers:

SPACE: You have an independent mind and like to think for yourself. You are not influenced by popular opinion.

CLINGING: When making decisions, you are influenced by commonly accepted opinions. You are also concerned with what others think.

Segment Groups

— — ∿∿ ☾ ∿∿ — —

With your palm faced toward you, look at your fingers. You will see that each one of your fingers is divided into three parts, or segments. You will notice dark, horizontal lines that divide each of the three segments from the others. The most important thing to notice is which segment group is the longest. One set of segments—the upper, middle, or lower—will always be longer than the others, even if only slightly.

Again, trust your first quick glance. The more hands you look at, the easier it will be to recognize which segment group is longer.

The segment groups let us know if the hands belong to intellectual, practical, or physical people.

LONG UPPER SEGMENTS: If your upper segments are the longest of the three, you are a thinker. You like to learn and collect information. People with longer uppers like to do things like play chess, read books, and solve puzzles. You also like to be around interesting people—people who can teach you things and who are full of ideas. You may enjoy history or social studies. News reports are also interesting to you because you like to know what is going on in the world. When you get older, you may want to teach or instruct others in some way.

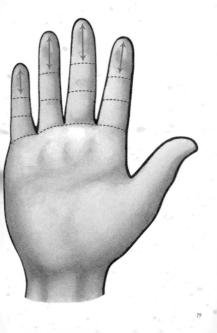

LONG MIDDLE SEGMENTS: Having the middle segments be the longest on your fingers shows that you are ambitious and like to achieve your goals. When you get older, you may want to become a businessperson, because you like money and what it will buy. Longer middles give a person a desire to own and collect things. Adults with long middles like to spend money, especially on things like cars, homes, and jewelry. People with long middles are neat and organized, with a place for everything.

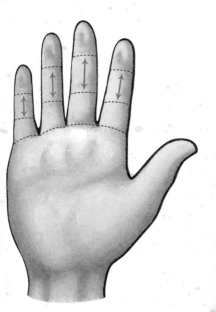

LONG LOWER SEGMENTS: If these are the longest segments of the three for you, then you have a physically strong and healthy body. You will always be active and energetic. It is common among those with long lowers to enjoy working with their hands. This could include fixing things, making things, or cooking. You will find that you like many things in your life to stay the way they are.

For example, you are happy to live in the same house or neighborhood for years. Too much moving and change is very difficult for you. Sticking to a daily schedule will help you to accomplish your goals.

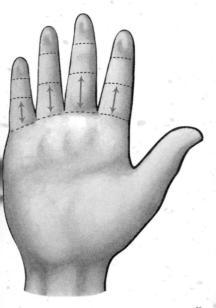

The Individual Segments

— — 〰〰 ☾ 〰〰 — —

Now we will look closely at each individual finger segment. Finger segments reveal our individual talents and abilities. Each finger is divided into three sections. Notice which segment on each finger is the longest. One segment will always be longer than the other two, even if only slightly, so look carefully. Once you've analyzed each finger, identify your longest segment of all twelve. This will specify your most powerful expertise.

Everyone will have one segment that stands out as the longest. You are now on a mission to find your strongest, or most important, finger segment. We call this the main segment.

Your main segment will let you know which are your strongest talents. Examine each of your segments closely and take your time to discover which of your segments is the longest. You might want to use a ruler on this one!

Jupiter Finger

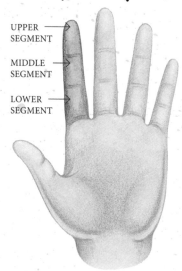

UPPER
SEGMENT

MIDDLE
SEGMENT

LOWER
SEGMENT

UPPER: Spirituality

You are a very spiritual person. You are interested in all kinds of spiritual activities. You may also have a little psychic ability.

KEY IDEAS:
- Strong Spiritual Aspirations
- Visionary and Idealistic
- Refined Emotions

MIDDLE: Ambition

You are ambitious. You like to accomplish big things and rise to the top. For example, if you're a lawyer, you will work harder longer than anybody else to be the best. You work hard to be the most successful.

KEY IDEAS:
- Entrepreneurial
- Business Leader
- Ambitious Achiever

LOWER: The Leader

You love being in charge of
people. Whether you are team
captain or class president, you like
it when people listen to you. You
also have a lot of self-confidence,
but watch that you don't become
egotistical.

> **KEY IDEAS:**
> - Coaching, Training,
>   and Managing Skills
> - Leadership with Heart

Saturn Finger

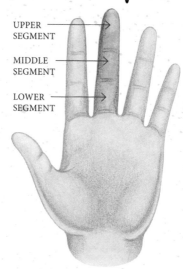

UPPER
SEGMENT

MIDDLE
SEGMENT

LOWER
SEGMENT

UPPER: Knowledge

You are an information addict. Learning and studying things is what you love to do. You may enjoy the History Channel or reading books on ancient civilizations.

KEY IDEAS:
- Student of Metaphysics, Magic, and Ancient Wisdom
- Philosophically Minded

MIDDLE: The Organizer

You are very good at organizing things. You have the ability to plan group activities and arrange for projects to go smoothly. You probably keep your room very neat and clean.

KEY IDEAS:
- Good Planner and Organizer
- Industrious
- Good Time Management

LOWER: The Environmentalist

You love the land and the Earth. You are into ecology and the environment. You can be found outdoors often, and you probably enjoy growing things.

> **KEY IDEAS:**
> - Strong Need for Security and Stability
> - Nature Lover

Sun Finger

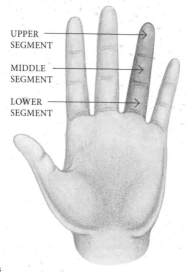

UPPER SEGMENT

MIDDLE SEGMENT

LOWER SEGMENT

UPPER: The Individualist

You are an individualist. You do not like to follow the crowd. You add your own personal style to everything that you do. You can also be a risk-taker.

> **KEY IDEAS:**
> - Has a Critic's Eye
> - Expert at Appraisal
> - Values Individuality

MIDDLE: The Artist

Artistic design and decoration
are your talents. Everything from
computer graphics to arts and crafts
interests you. Whether you like to
design clothes or draw cartoons, you
are a very creative person.

KEY IDEAS:
- Social Magnetism
- Talent for
  Presentation Arts
- Design, Decoration,
  or Fashion Sense

LOWER: The Entertainer

You love to be popular and the center of attention. You tend to be very fashionably dressed. You may enjoy being an actor or a musician.

KEY IDEAS:
- Competent in Physical Activities
- Concerned with Appearance
- Has Performance Skills

Mercury Finger

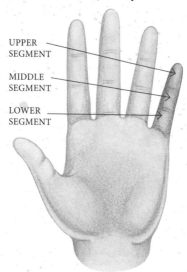

UPPER
SEGMENT

MIDDLE
SEGMENT

LOWER
SEGMENT

UPPER: The Communicator

You love to talk! You have the ability to express yourself well and might enjoy public speaking. You may also spend a lot of time on the telephone.

> **KEY IDEAS:**
> - Has an Inventive and Ingenious Mind
> - An Abstract and Conceptual Thinker

MIDDLE: The Writer

You have a natural ability to write. You are very curious and always ask questions. You may be interested in investigative reporting.

KEY IDEAS:
- Good Communicator
- Interested in Media Work
- Advertising or Marketing Ability

LOWER: Technology

You love all types of technology. This includes electronics and mechanics. Work with computers and gadgets!

> **KEY IDEAS:**
> - Good Technical Skills
> - Interest in How Things Work

Fingerprints

— ∿∿ ☾ ∿∿ —

Everyone knows that the police use fingerprints to identify people. However, only palmists know that the waves and lines on our fingertips can also tell us our life path.

Palmistry structures human society according to four different paths of nature. By following our life path, we follow our own true natures. Our talents and abilities will quickly come alive when we are aware of our life path.

The life path is your special challenge in this life, one that you met and did not complete in your previous incarnations. Life will be easier when you follow your life path.

There are four different types of fingerprints. They are:

	The Wave Life Path: Responsibility
	The Tent Life Path: Courage
	The Comet Life Path: The Heart
	The Whirlpool Life Path: Teacher

Now look closely at all of your fingers, including your thumb. This is highly meticulous, up-close work, so make sure that you're doing your palmistry reading in light that's bright enough for you to see all of the details of the fingerprints in front of you. You can also use a magnifying glass for this if you need to.

Carefully decide whether you have a Wave, Tent, Comet, or Whirlpool as the dominant feature on each finger—and remember, each finger can only have one type of fingerprint. Next, write down the fingerprint type of each finger on a piece of paper, and count them up to determine your life path.

If you have 2 or more Waves, your life path is **RESPONSIBILITY**.

☽

If you have 2 or more Tents, your life path is **COURAGE**.

☽

If you have 4 or more Whirlpools, your life path is **THE TEACHER**.

☽

If you have 7 or more Comets, your life path is **THE HEART**.

RESPONSIBILITY

— — ∿∿∿ ☾ ∿∿∿ — —

Your life path is to be a responsible
person. In the duties that are given to
you, or that you take on yourself, you
will become a strong person by being
productive and working hard at what
you do. Those that have this life path
have difficulty feeling inner peace.
They get restless easily if they are not
self-disciplined. Even if you have difficulties, you will be able to deal with life
easily and stay calm if you take pride in
your work and do it well. Also, being in
nature makes you feel relaxed. Walking
through a forest, working outdoors, or
even working in a garden will make you
feel happy and fulfilled.

THE HEART

— ∿∿ ☾ ∿∿ —

Your life path is to put your heart into everything that you do. You are happiest when you can express your feelings and your dreams. The things that you do the best are the things that you can put your heart and imagination into. Always let others know how you are feeling. If you hide your emotions, life will be very difficult. Also, you may enjoy writing, because it's a good way for you to bring out your feelings, ideas, and dreams.

Those with the Heart Path tend to be emotional people. Being an emotionally driven person is not a problem, but people on this path worry that if they express their love and feelings for others, they will be rejected. This is rarely how others react, so have the courage to show your feelings and express your love without fear. It takes strength to be loving and honest, so be strong!

COURAGE

—— 〰 ☾ 〰 ——

Your life path is to always be a go-getter. This means that if you are an enthusiastic person, things will always work out for you. You have the ability to start projects on your own and make things happen. Always remember that things will not go your way if you lack determination or do not take action. You also have the ability to motivate and inspire people—you could organize a large meeting, a protest march, or a charity drive. This life path provides a special ability to develop the qualities of courage and bravery. So, whether in physical or intellectual activities, never hesitate to take a stand and act boldly.

THE TEACHER

— — ∿∿∿ ☾ ∿∿∿ — —

Your life path is to help others to learn. This means that when you are good at something, you should share it or teach it to others. For example, if you enjoy playing a sport, you should teach others how to play it. If you write a story, you should end it with a message. You are good at coming up with new ideas and sharing them. You like it when people come to you for advice, but you can become upset when they do not listen. This should not discourage you from helping others to learn.

In past ages, those with this life path often held various positions as advisers to the king and queen. You are on the planet to acquire knowledge, in order to eventually give guidance and direction to society.

PART III:
THE THUMB

×△×

Thumb Shapes

— —〰〰 ☾ 〰〰— —

Our palm and fingers contain our talents and abilities. Our thumb is like the engine that can make those talents come to life.

It is only by looking at lots of hands that you will be able to decide if a thumb is fat, thin, long, or short. Don't worry if this part is a bit difficult to figure out. If you look at enough hands, it will be easy, in time.

These are the four paradigms for the thumb:

FAT THUMBS:
Indicate an outgoing and aggressive nature.

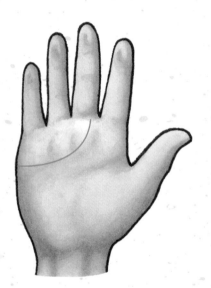

CURVED JUPITER: You put your feelings and emotions into your friends and those you love. In order for you to get things done, it is important for you to work in a peaceful and quiet area. You like to work with others, but only if it is with people that you know very well. You prefer to work in small groups. Getting along with people is important to you, and you hate fighting and arguing. You can be a very dependable friend, and you expect your friends to be loyal to you.

When someone around you is sick or needs some kind of help, you're always there for them. Many people who love and care for animals also have this Water Line pattern.

THIN THUMBS:
Mean that a
person is quiet
and shy.

LONG THUMBS:
Show the owner
does things slowly
and carefully.

SHORT THUMBS:
Belong to those
who do things
quickly and
immediately.

Symmetrical vs. Synchronistic Thumbs

—— ∿∿ ☾ ∾∾ ——

If observed from the nail side, a thumb's width generally remains uniform beginning from its base to the beginning of the nail. This is called the Symmetrical Thumb. Owners of this thumb have a strong belief that opportunities will only present themselves if they actively pursue them. Therefore, they have no trouble making decisions.

Some thumbs have a shape in which the area between the base and the knuckle is indented on both sides. This called the Synchronistic Thumb. This signifies an inner faith that life unfolds according to a transcendent plan.

People who have it have faith that the forces of nature present opportunities to them. The good news is that these people possess the quality of patience and have a natural spiritual outlook. The bad news is that they could be behind in making decisions for themselves. Consequently, they must learn to act on life as much as possible, rather than continue allowing life to act on them.

Thumb Position

—— ∿∿∿ ☾ ∿∿∿ ——

Are you an intuitive thinker? Or are
you an analytical one? This exercise
will determine whether it is the head
or the heart that ultimately influences
your consciousness and your actions
in life. Clasp your hands together
and note which thumb has landed on
top of the other. If the left thumb
naturally lands on top, you are a
right-brained thinker. If the right
thumb lands on top, then you are a
left-brained thinker.

Left Brain:	**Right Brain:**
· Analytical	· Intuitive
· Objective	· Subjective
· Logical	· Dreamy
· Reasonable	· Creative
· Calculating	· Holistically
· Practical	Imaginative

Thumb Placement:

— — ᐯᐯᐯ ᗕ ᐯᐯᐯ — —

Relax your hands by shaking them.
Then place them palm down on a table.
Now look at your thumbs. How far
apart do your thumbs stick out from
your palm and fingers?

FAR OUT: If your thumb sticks way
out, you are a very confident person.
You like to depend
on yourself and
make your
own decisions.
You especially
enjoy being in
charge of things
and people. You
also like to be a
leader. Try not
to be too bossy!

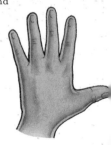

MODERATE: If your thumb sticks out halfway, you need freedom. You are not as interested in being in charge of others, and you like personal independence. It is easy for you to get along with others. You also like working with a group or a team.

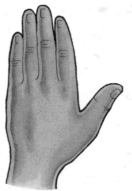

CLOSE: Does your thumb stay close to the palm? If it does, it means that you like to keep to yourself a lot. Actually, you will find that you get things done better when you are alone. Being around loud people, or people who tell you what to do, is very annoying. Try to be more social or outgoing if possible. And if you're asked to take on more responsibility, try to do it.

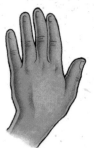

TOUCHING: When you place your hands down on a table, do your thumbs touch your palms, or even curl within it? You need to become more confident! It is important that you tell your feelings and problems to your parents and those you love and trust. Learn to feel that you can accomplish things if you try hard. Also, try to have a more positive attitude.

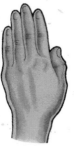

Thumb Set

—— ∿∿∿ ☾ ∿∿∿ ——

The thumb can be attached anywhere from the base of the palm at the wrist to the middle of the palm toward the fingers. The placement of the thumb at the border of the palm is significant because it reveals the direction of your occupational proclivity.

LOW: Those with low-set thumbs are practical achievers.

KEY IDEAS:
- Achieves Tangible, Concrete Results
- Enjoys Mechanical/Technical Endeavors
- Likes to Build and Create
- Good Architects, Illustrators, Surgeons, and Musicians

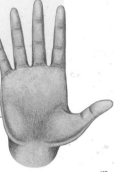

HIGH: A high-set thumb denotes a mental achiever.

KEY IDEAS:
- Achievers in the World of Ideas and Concepts
- Enjoys Brainstorming and Problem Solving
- Likes Mental Challenges
- Writers, Researchers, Psychologists, Teachers, Consultants

The Thumb's Segments

Our thumb is divided into three segments. Which part of your thumb is the longest? If one or two segments are longer than the others, those energies will be stronger for you.

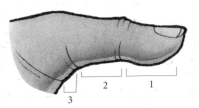

The First Segment: EGO

—— 〜〜〜 (〜〜〜 ——

The top segment of the thumb represents how much control and influence we have over our environment. This section should be as long or longer than the second segment. It should also feel well-padded and firm to the touch. A segment like this shows the ability to create and shape one's surroundings and to make things happen. It also gives one the ability to influence others. Segments that are very long or large show that one can be stubborn and may wish to dominate situations. A strong first segment reveals an ability to achieve results through effort.

A person with a short or flattened segment does not have the same ability to have a strong effect on their surroundings. Quite often, the area will also feel soft. This adds to the segment's weakness. A person with a weak segment will feel overwhelmed and frustrated because they have difficulty in achieving results. What if your segment is not strong? You may feel that even if you do work hard, success will not come. Learn to break this negative thinking pattern and your first segment will strengthen.

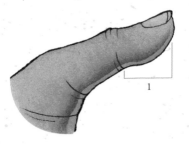

1

The Second Segment:
INTELLIGENCE

— — ᨓᨓ ☾ ᨓᨓ — —

The second segment represents the
ability to make decisions for yourself.
A middle segment that is longer than
the other two reveals that you are constantly thinking about what actions to
take. You also love to give advice. You
feel good when you are asked to help
make choices for others. You are always
coming up with plans and ideas. If this
segment looks the smallest to you, it
means that you are shy about making
decisions and plans for yourself.
Learn to trust your own decisions
and judgments.

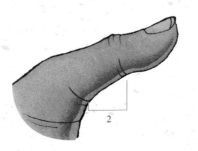

2

The Third Segment:
THE MIND

—— ∧∧∧ ☾ ∨∨∨ ——

This segment indicates how much determination you have. A good length shows that you can concentrate on your own talents and desires in order to achieve them. It could take the form of a creative or communicative ability. For example, if you have a good imagination, it could be practically applied to some form of art. Or, if you have good speaking skills, you wouldn't be afraid to give a speech or express an opinion.

Sometimes this segment is hard to find, or it can look like the thumb has only two segments instead of three. This means that the drive and determination to bring out one's own personal desires and abilities needs to be developed. This particular section of the thumb is the most "changeable" on the hand. If your third segment is weak, remember that goals are easily achieved by making the mind stronger and using its powers of concentration. If you do this, your third segment will enlarge.

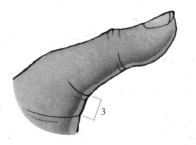

Flexibility

— ∼∼∼ ☾ ∼∼∼ —

Thumb flexibility is a gauge that measures the strength of your determination to achieve goals. Applying slight pressure to the upper section of the thumb, note its degree of reverse curvature.

RIGID: A thumb that remains inflexible with no noticeable arc indicates one who unwaveringly pursues their desires. The greater the arching of the upper section, the more adamant you must become to accomplish your aims.

Those with stiff thumbs pride themselves on following through on their commitments. They also like to have a voice in the affairs around them, and are not easily influenced by others.

KEY IDEAS:
- Resolute in Ideas and Views
- Frugal with Time, Energy, and Money
- Strong-Minded, May Be Stubborn
- Self-Reliant and Persistent

FLEXIBLE: Those with pliable thumbs are generous with their time, energy, and even money. They're also able to easily acclimate themselves to various different situations and even challenges. Those with considerable curvature must become more persistent to achieve their own aspirations, as their desires often get mixed up with the desires of others.

KEY IDEAS:
- Easy-Going and Helpful
- Cooperative and Persuadable
- Adaptable
- The Greater the Arc, the Weaker One's Will

PART IV: LINES

— ⚹ △ ⚹ —

Busy vs. Peaceful Hands

— — ∿∿∿ ☾ ∿∿∿ — —

Sometimes, a hand may be filled with lines going in every direction (#5), and it looks complicated! Palmists call this "the busy hand."

People who have many lines covering their palm have many different interests and hobbies. They like to know something about everything. Their minds are always alert to things that are going on around them. Sometimes they may find it difficult to concentrate on just one subject or hobby. They are interested in so many different things that they scatter their energy in too many directions.

If you have this palm pattern, try focusing on one or two subjects that really interest you.

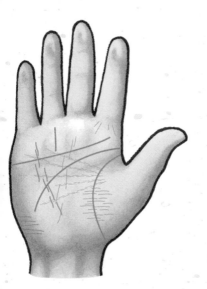

You may come across a palm that seems to have only three or four lines. These few lines are usually deeply cut into the hand. These are also darker in color than those of the busy hand. This hand is called "the peaceful hand" because it has fewer lines.

Focusing on one or two hobbies is not difficult for those with a peaceful hand. They know what they like to do, and they do it. These people are not really interested in what the rest of the world does or in other people's ideas.

If you have this palm pattern, try to keep your mind open to other's ideas and opinions. Take in those external ideas, and you will see that whatever you do well, you will soon be able to do even better!

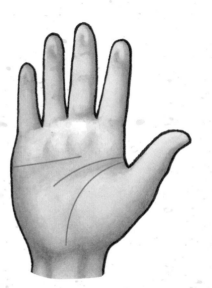

Type of Line

—— ∿∿ ☾ ∿∿ ——

Before we get into the meanings of
the individual lines, you should know
about a couple of overall characteristics
to take into consideration.

Deep vs. Shallow Lines

In palmistry, it's common to describe
the lines of the hand as a map of your
consciousness. Think of each line as
a flowing river. The deeper and wider
the line, the more power it can give
you, and the stronger its energy will be
in your life.

For example, if your line of Air is
deep, it shows that you spend much
time in thought (#1).

A shallow or narrow line shows less power in that area. If your line of Air looks light and skinny, it means that you have difficulty concentrating on your plans (#2).

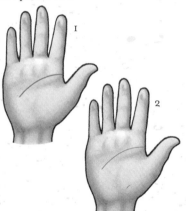

Clear vs. Blocked Lines

Like a river, a line should also look clear and clean. If it does, it will be easy for you and your life to express the meaning of that line. For example, if your line of Mercury looks clear, it will be easy for you to communicate your thoughts (#3).

A line can also have its path blocked, like a river with many logs or branches in its path. If so, it will be harder to express the energy of that line. For example, a line of Mercury with blockages (crossing lines) will show that you are hesitant to communicate your thoughts (#4).

If you always think of the lines as rivers of energy, understanding them

will be easy. Remember: When looking
at the lines in your palm, be sure to
concentrate more on your main hand.

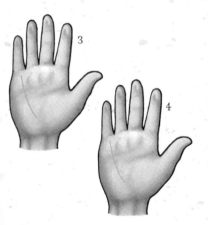

The 14 Lines

— — ∿∿∿ ☾ ∿∿∿ — —

While the world's various palm-reading
traditions view the hands in slightly
different ways, one commonality is
the importance of the basic fourteen
lines commonly found on the palm.
Knowing just these lines will give you
a good foundation in the basics of
palmistry, and help you inestimably in
giving palmistry readings to yourself
and others. Here is a quick guide to the
lines and their different meanings:

The Line of Earth: Lifestyle

The Line of Water: Emotions

The Line of Fire: Energy

The Line of Air: Thinking

The Union Line: Focus

The Lines of Jupiter: Spirituality

The Line of Saturn: Effort

The Line of the Sun: Optimism

The Line of Mercury: Communication

The Lines of Venus: Enjoyment

The Line of the Moon: Psychic Ability

The Lines of Mars: Courage

The Line of Neptune: Sensitivity

The Line of Icarus: Freedom

The Line of Earth

— — ∿∿ ☾ ∿∿ — —

People who know a little bit about palmistry call this the Life Line. The correct name is the Earth Line. Some people think that this line tells how long a person will live, but that's not actually true. The line of Earth shows how you want to live your life, not how long it will be.

A deep Earth Line grants the ability to peacefully handle the difficulties and struggles that one meets in life. A person with a shallow Earth Line tends to feel overwhelmed and unsettled when dealing with life's stresses and obstacles. Also, keep in mind that the deeper or wider the line of Earth, the more physical strength a person will have. A shallow or narrow line will show a lesser amount of physical strength.

The line of Earth always starts from the middle of the palm (on the thumb side), and moves down the hand. The place that the line ends is also very important to its meaning. The line of Earth curves around the ball of the thumb, circumscribing the area called the Mountain of Venus.

We will now look at the six basic Earth Line patterns over the pages that follow. As you examine these pages, look at the patterns to compare them to your hands and discover which Earth Line you have. Remember to primarily look at your main hand.

OUTGOING: This type of Earth Line has a curve that is large and fat. The curve almost reaches the middle of the palm. Having this Earth Line means that you are a very outgoing person. You rarely wish to do things alone, or just be by yourself at home. You most often like to be outside, engaged in activities with your friends.

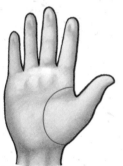

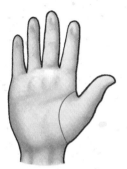

HOMEBODY: This is an Earth Line that does not curve that far into the palm, but stays close to the thumb. This line will be closer to straight, rather than forming a wide curve. This type of line means that being around crowds is not your thing. You like a lot of peace and quiet. You do need to socialize at times, but not too much. You are content with a few good friends.

FAMILY PERSON: If your Earth Line ends at the bottom of the Mountain of Venus, you will find that your home and family are extremely important to you. You like a comfortable bedroom and you enjoy decorating it and spending time there. You do not like moving too often. The neighborhood that you live in is also very important to you. You always have a need to know what's going on around your town. You might live in the countryside, or want to move there some day.

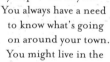

ADVENTURER: This Earth Line travels farther toward the other side of the palm, and ends on the Mountain of the Moon. If the line on your palm does this, you love all types of adventure and travel. You would much rather spend time investigating the world than hang out around your neighborhood or your home. You might want to become an archaeologist or an explorer. You probably enjoy going on long trips and journeys. Reading about distant places and people also interests you.

RESTLESS: A short Earth Line means that a person likes a lot of freedom. Owners of this line are restless and enjoy working hard. If you have this line, you might find that you spend a lot of time and energy working toward a goal. A person training hard for the Olympics might also have this line. Most commonly, those who have this short line will put the bulk of their time and energy into their career. They want to be successful. Sometimes they can work too hard, though—they need to learn to relax and enjoy themselves.

CHANGES OF LIFESTYLE: This line will travel halfway around the Mountain of Venus and then stop. It will then begin again in a close, but different, place. Every time your Earth Line breaks, you will move to a different place. If the break is large, you may make a big move that changes your whole life. This may be like moving from the East Coast to the West Coast. If your Earth Line has two or three such breaks, it shows that you have the ability to handle these immense changes.

The Line of Water

— ∿∿ ☾ ∿∿ —

The line of Water is sometimes called the Heart Line. It is the upper horizontal line on the palm, found just below the fingers. This line always starts from the Mercury Finger side of the palm, and travels toward the thumb side. This line tells us about our feelings, our emotions, and what in life we put our heart into. The most important thing to notice about this line is whether it is straight or curved.

Those who have curved Water Lines have the ability and the need to express their feelings and emotions. People whose Water Lines are straight also have strong feelings inside, but they have a harder time talking about them.

CURVED: If your Water Line curves, you like to express what is in your heart. You have a strong need to always share your feelings and emotions with others. If you like to write, the topics tend to be who and what you love. If something is bothering you, you need to let others know about it and not hold it in.

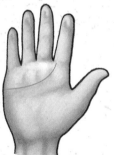

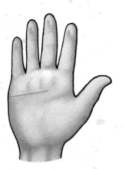

STRAIGHT: When you talk to others, you express what is going on in your mind, rather than your heart. You may have difficulty discussing your feelings with others, but you are comfortable expressing your thoughts and ideas. Try not to be shy about letting other people know how you are feeling, rather than just what you are thinking.

Now we will look at four of the most important Water Line endings. Look at your palm to see which one of these you have.

STRAIGHT SATURN: You put your feelings and emotions into becoming a strong, self-confident, and independent person. You enjoy working alone, rather than with others. You are also able to get more things done when you do them by yourself. You are a very independent person, and you like to have freedom. You do need to socialize sometimes, but not as much as others. You're the type of person that loves to have your own special, private place. It is hard for you to express your feelings to others. Do not be shy about expressing them from time to time.

You do have a warm heart, but you hold back and keep a lot inside. If you don't express your feelings at all, you will feel that others don't understand you.

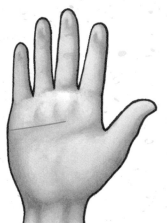

CURVED SATURN: You put your feelings and emotions into enjoying life, being active, and becoming a leader. When you do things with other people, you like to be the leader of the group. You also do not like to follow the rules of others. Your friends will listen to what you have to say when you are in charge. You also like to be the center of attention. You get bored very easily if you are around dull and uninteresting people. You like to attend loud parties and amusement parks, and to play challenging sports.

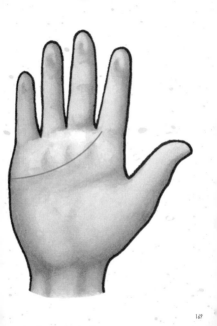

STRAIGHT JUPITER: You put your emotions and feelings into helping humanity. You love working with large groups of people, and you always enjoy meeting new people and making friends. It is easy for you to share and cooperate with others. You are also good at bringing people together. You will find that your friends will easily tell you about their feelings and problems. This Water Line pattern ensures that you can give good advice, and you love doing it! This is because you have a talent for analyzing emotions. Many psychologists have this shape of Water Line. People who become doctors, healers, or astrologers also often have this line, having entered their professions because they enjoy helping others.

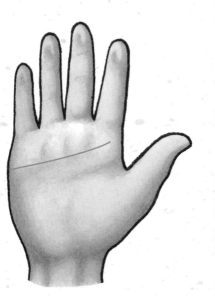

The Line of Fire

—— ∧∧∧ ☾ ∨∨∨ ——

The Fire Line is one of the most
important lines on your palm. If this
line is present—which isn't always
the case—it sits just behind the Earth
Line. Fire itself attracts us. It is bright,
intense, and always moving—a blazing
fire draws us in like a magnet, and
has since throughout the history of
humankind. Therefore, anyone who
has this line will be full of life. You
want to be around them because they
are fun and exciting to be with.

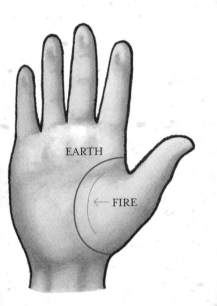

EARTH

← FIRE

People who have a line of Fire have the element of Fire within them. This Fire energy makes a person always active and busy. This line does not give physical energy—that's the job of the Earth Line—but it gives more of a restless energy. Just as Fire is always restless and does not want to stay in one place, owners of this line can't stay still for very long.

They always have to be doing something. You do not need to have a long and deep line of Fire to own this fire energy. Most people will have one or two little pieces of it. This line is so powerful that you only need a very small part of it for it to do its job. After all, one small flame can start a giant fire.

A deep line of Fire can make you an enthusiastic person who's very motivated to accomplish things. It gives you the needed energy to get things going. Think of a stick of dynamite: It has the power to cause a large explosion, but it's harmless without the strike of a match. The Fire Line is like our match. Some people do not have any trace of this line. This means that they may have the desire or the physical strength to do things, but they may be lazy or uninspired. Having a Fire Line will give one the energy necessary to get things started. If you see a friend who does not seem to have this line, encourage them to become more enthusiastic. If they do, the line will slowly begin to appear.

The Line of Air

—— ᠕᠕᠕ ☾ ᠕᠕᠕ ——

The line of Air is the horizontal line
in the middle of the palm. It starts
from the thumb side of the hand, and
travels toward the side of the Mercury
Finger. Air (or wind) carries sound,
which carries information and ideas.
For example, humans and most animals
communicate their thoughts and ideas
by sound, which is carried through
the air. So, this line of Air carries
our thoughts, ideas, and interests. It
explains how we think and what we
think about.

There are two things to consider
with the line of Air: the shape and the
length. If our brain is a computer,

then the shape of the line shows us what kind of computer we own. The length of the line will show us how we use our computer.

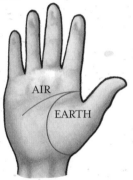

AIR

EARTH

There are four main Air Line shapes. Look at them all, and decide which one you have.

STRAIGHT: Does your line of Air travel straight? If so, you are a logical thinker. You base most of your thinking and views on facts and information. For you to believe in something, it has to be proven to you. You are also very good at analyzing things and thinking them through step-by-step. You will find this line on many scientific researchers and inventors.

The straight line is also common among those who enjoy working with technology and mathematical formulas. Owning this line means that you like to read things that give you information and knowledge. You like nonfiction and how-to books. For you like a book of fiction at all, it usually has to be based on real-life events. You also have the ability to observe and study facts, which is why most detectives have this type of line.

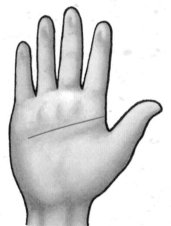

SLIGHTLY CURVED: Does your line of Air curve down slightly? If so, you are a creative thinker. You base a lot of your thinking on what you wish for and how you would like things to be. You have many original ideas. People who have curved Air Lines enjoy being artists, musicians, and actors. Many movie directors also have this line pattern. This line is also an indicator of a person who can design and create things, such as clothing, cars, and houses.

You also love variety in your life! For example, you may meet people who only like a certain type of music, and no other—but that's not you. If you like music, you will enjoy listening to everything. You have a very open mind and can be inspired by many different things.

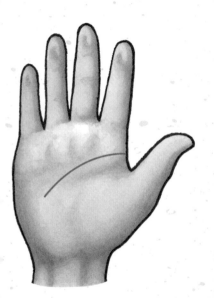

STRONGLY CURVED: Does your line of Air strongly curve down? If so, you have a strong and colorful imagination. You spend much time dreaming, night and day. If you try writing or drawing, you'll be able to create amazing fantasy. Many science fiction, romance, and fantasy artists and writers have this type of line. There is also a moody side to you. When you feel moody, try writing down your thoughts: You'll learn a lot about yourself and your emotions by doing so.

There is also a very spiritual side to you. It is easy for you to accept that spiritual forces are at work in the world. You are always on the lookout to see spiritual reasons behind events that take place. You are not the type who believes that things just happen by chance. People with this line also often become interested in legends from the ancient world, such as Greek or Egyptian mythologies.

You have the ability to trust your inner voice. The inner voice is a feeling from inside that lets you know what you should or should not do, and you're right to trust it. If you listen to it, it can help you to make the right decisions. This feeling is also called intuition.

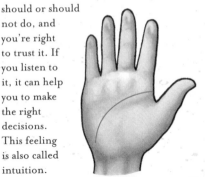

CURVED UP: Does your line of Air curve up? If so, you are a practical thinker. You think in a very down-to-earth way.

To you, things have to be realistic, rather than imaginative. For example, you like art that shows things the way they are, not someone's fantasy. You have a very sharp or shrewd mind. This means that if you have to buy something, you make sure to get the best price, and you rarely get cheated. This pattern also shows an ability to make money and spend it wisely. People with this line are great at starting new companies and businesses. You will often see it on bankers and successful businesspeople.

You would love being part of a debate team. You have the ability to fully understand another person's point of view, and then defeat them using their own argument! That's why the best lawyers always have this line.

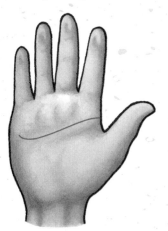

Air Line Lengths

There are three main Air Line lengths. Look at them all, and decide which one you have.

SECTION A: If your Air Line ends within section A, under the finger of Saturn, your mind thinks in the present. When deciding to do something, you trust the first thought that comes to you, or your first idea. You are not interested in what has happened in the past, and you will deal with the future when it comes. Therefore, you have the ability to make decisions immediately and you can give quick answers. When asked a question, you almost never say, "Maybe" or "Give me time to think about it." And if someone insults you, you will always have a fast comeback line.

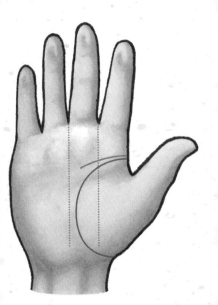

SECTION B: Those who have the section B ending, under the Sun Finger, put a lot of thought into making plans for the future. For example, if they earn money, they will not spend it immediately. They will take time to think about how they are going to spend it, and tend to save more than people with other line endings. If you have this Air Line length, you will put a lot of time training or working toward your future goals. That work could be something like practicing on an instrument or training for a sport for several hours a day. You like to have fun, but you will always be very serious about your ambitions.

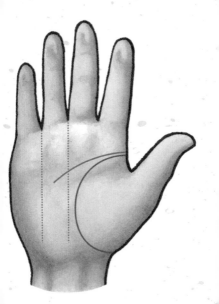

SECTION C: If you have the section C ending, under the finger of Mercury, you make your decisions based upon your past experiences. If asked a question, you will always think about your answer carefully. This is because you consider experiences that have happened in the past before deciding what to do in the future. You don't like to be rushed into making plans. You have a mind that can take in a lot of information. Therefore, you put a lot of thought into the things that you do.

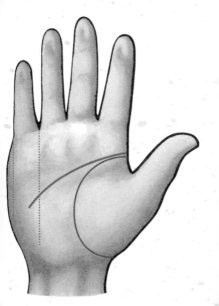

The Union Line

—— ∿∿∿ ☾ ∿∿∿ ——

Occasionally, you will find a palm that shows the Air Line and the Heart Line merged together. It is not uncommon to find this line, but it is rare to find it on both palms. When the lines are separated and do not touch each other, they have the ability to bring out their full power. Lines that begin and end independently act like radars. Just as a radar can send out and pick up signals and information, an independent line can properly express and receive energies. However, a line that runs into or combines with another line will lose this radar-like ability.

A person with such a line has difficulty communicating their internal thoughts and feelings. This is combined with a lack of ability to understand the psychology of others. Relating to people and forming strong friendships is a challenge for these people. They find it easier to stay in their own world, and consequently, they often end up feeling lonely and isolated. If you have this line, take the time to inquire about the thoughts and feelings of your friends. Make more of an effort to clearly explain what is going on inside of you. If you do this, you will feel much more harmony in your life.

The Union Line does have a positive side. Those with it have the ability to focus and concentrate on a goal without letting anything distract them. You will find this line on successful politicians, entertainers, and businesspeople—the ones who do not let anything get in the way of achieving their goals. When the Air and Water Lines run together, their owner becomes emotionally involved in everything that they think about, meaning that they commit to things to a truly impressive degree, because they care so deeply about the things that they direct their mental energy toward. The result is that such people are able to strongly and persistently focus on their interests, because the mind and the heart act as one.

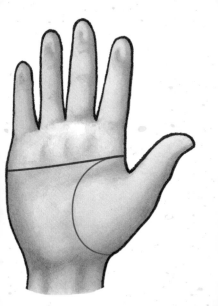

The Lines of Jupiter

—— ∿∿∿ ☾ ∿∿∿ ——

The Lines of Jupiter are lines of spiritual and mystical awareness. These lines can be found on the upper part of the Mountain of Jupiter, just below the finger of Jupiter. They will usually be narrow and short. Look at this area very closely. These lines can be very light and difficult to see.

All lines in this area are lines of spirituality. If you have them, it means that you had an interest in mystical or spiritual things in your past lives. And if you have one strong line directly under the finger of Jupiter, it means that in your past lives, you prayed to and worshiped God as a person, rather than as an energy or a force.

If you continue your spiritual path, these lines will get longer, deeper, and stronger. What if you do not have any lines in this area? Do not worry—they will appear and grow if you become interested in a spiritual path.

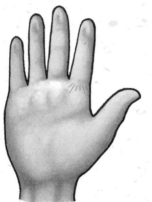

The Line of Saturn

— ∿∿ ☾ ∿∿ —

This line starts out at the bottom of the palm and travels toward the finger of Saturn. It is easy to find because it is the vertical line that runs through the center of the palm. That said, it will not always be a straight line. This line shows that one has the ability to make an effort. A person who has it will try very hard to accomplish things. It's a very important line to have.

If you have this line, it means that you take time to do things that need to be done. You work at things that are expected of you, like your job, schooling or duties at home. This can also include a hobby that you work hard at. You may sometimes see palms that do not have a Saturn Line, or it may be so light and narrow that it is hard to see.

This means that the person does not try hard enough at what needs to be done or what is expected of them. They may waste a lot of their time or relax too much. If you see someone without this important line, encourage them to be more serious about their responsibilities.

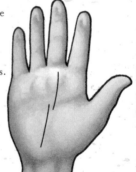

The Line of the Sun

—— ∿∿ ☾ ∿∿ ——

This line appears on the Mountain of
the Sun, under the finger of the Sun. It
is usually found above the line of Water.
It is usually not very long. There can
also be a number of short Sun Lines in
the same space instead. This will almost
be the same as having one line.

This line does not have to be
strongly cut into your palm. This is a
powerful line, and you only need to
have a small bit of it in order for the
Sun energy to come through. Do not
worry if your line or lines are light and
narrow. The Sun makes us happy and
joyful when it shines brightly on us,
especially if the world has been dark
and cloudy for a long time.

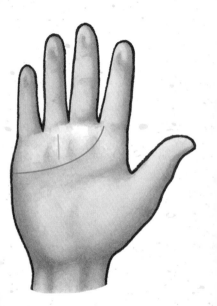

The line of the Sun gives us this bright Sun energy. Having this line means that you are able to be positive. Those with a Sun Line do not get discouraged or disappointed easily. Even if they are having a bad day, they do not let it get them down for very long. They just know that everything will soon work out for them. If you have a Sun Line, you are able to help your friends feel better when they are feeling sad or upset.

Just as you cannot ignore the Sun on a hot day, those owning a Sun Line naturally attract people. They are noticed and remembered. If you ever have the chance to read the hands of popular entertainers, check out their Sun Line. The longer and deeper their line, the longer they will stay popular.

What if you have no Sun Line at all?
Try to develop a positive attitude, and
never give up. Learn to see that any
difficulties that you go through should
not discourage you, because they will
help to make you a stronger person.
If you do this, the line of the Sun will
start to grow on your hand.

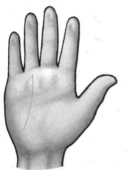

The Line of Mercury

—— ∿∿∿ ☾ ∨∨∨ ——

The line of Mercury is found on the Mercury Finger side of the palm. It is easy to identify because it is the only vertical line that heads toward the finger of Mercury. The line shows that you can and want to communicate through writing and speaking. Many people can communicate or speak well, but not everybody has a strong need to express their own views in this fashion.

If you have this line, being able to express your opinions is very important to you. Most people, for example, will be able to tell you what they heard on a news report, but a person with a Mercury Line will give you the news *and* their opinion on it.

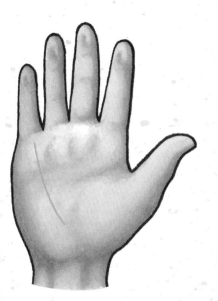

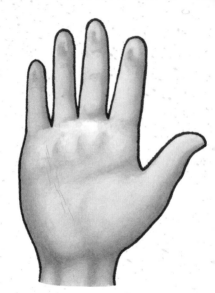

What if you have a Mercury Line, but it is broken up or very light? This means that you want to express your opinions, but you're holding yourself back. Often, you're holding back because you feel that people would not take your thoughts or opinions seriously if you did share them. Don't worry about this; express your ideas to people anyway, and your line will grow strong and deep.

What if there is no line of Mercury on your hand? Writing might be a good way to form and become familiar with your thoughts and opinions.

The Lines of Venus

—— ∿∿∿ ☾ ∨∨∨ ——

The lines of Venus are short horizontal lines on the Mountain of Venus. On this area, you can have either three or four strong lines, or many little ones.

These lines mean that you love to play around, laugh, and enjoy yourself. You also like to entertain others, go to parties, and socialize. You have a serious side, but you also need to have fun. The more lines of Venus that you have, the more enjoyment you will seek out. So if the mountain on someone's palm is completely covered with Venus Lines, that person will be a party animal.

If the Venus Lines are hard to find, it means that the person's enjoying spirit is not very strong. Someone with a hand like that may rarely be interested in socializing and playing around.

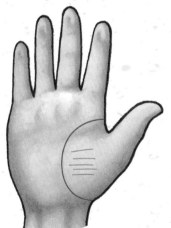

The Line of the Moon

— ∿∿ ☾ ∿∿ —

This line usually forms a half-circle on the Mountain of the Moon. To have it is to have true psychic power. You may even have the ability to know what will happen in the future. Owners of the line of the Moon seem to know who is calling them when the phone rings. It can also give one the power to read others' thoughts or know what people are going to say before they say it. If you have this line, try working with the Tarot cards, and your psychic ability may become strong.

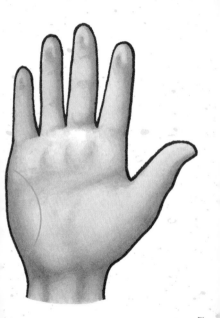

The Lines of Mars

— ∿∿ ☾ ∿∿ —

These lines start out on the Mountain of Mars and move out into the rest of the palm. These lines make one competitive and aggressive. People who own deep Mars Lines use their competitiveness in a physical way. You will often find these lines on professional athletes. If the Mars Lines are very deep, they show one who is courageous and brave. Firefighters, for example, tend to have very deep Mars lines.

Mars Lines that are more shallow and narrow belong to people who are competitive and aggressive with their mind and thoughts. They can use this competitive energy in a career such as news reporting, politics, or business. When you see these Mars Lines, remember that they add an extra measure of boldness to a person's life.

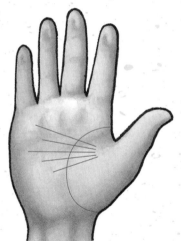

The Line of Neptune

—— ᙏᙏ ☾ ᙎᙎ ——

The line of Neptune is a small half-circle line at the very top of the palm. Having this line on your palm shows that you are always warm and friendly to others. You are also sensitive to the world around you. The people around you and the places you go often influence your moods. It also bothers you to see people or animals suffer. Therefore, you will want a career in which you can help others. You might enjoy working with animals. Arguments and fights disturb those with the line of Neptune; they are pleased when people around them cooperate and work together.

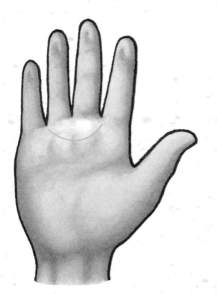

The Line of Icarus

——〜〜〜 ☾ 〜〜〜 ——

In ancient Greek mythology, Icarus
and his father, Daedalus, escaped from
prison by using wings made of feathers
and wax. As Daedalus flew on to
freedom, Icarus grew so excited with his
freedom and his ability to soar across
the sky, that he flew higher and higher,
until the heat from the sun melted the
wax holding his wings together, and
he fell to the earth. This line is named
after Icarus because it symbolizes a
need for freedom and excitement. As
human beings, we need to know that
we have a certain amount of freedom
and independence in our lives in order
to be happy and peaceful. Those with
the line of Icarus have a constant need

to break free from restrictions and limitations imposed upon them—even if acting on that need has negative consequences, as it ultimately did for Icarus at the end of the myth.

They may constantly push themselves to do things better than they have before. They strongly dislike living in a society that limits their freedom. They value independence and rarely follow the crowd unless it suits their own desire. They are never people who become blind followers, going along with what is commonly accepted.

There are four different types of Icarus Lines:

SHORT: These lines start from the edge of the Moon Mountain. They are short lines, usually about one inch in length. Having one to four lines shows that the person likes a life in which they can have a different schedule every day. They do not like routines. A person with five or more lines gets bored very easily and likes constant change. They enjoy traveling and visiting new places.

MOON TO SATURN: If the line of
Icarus starts from the Moon Mountain
and connects to the Saturn Line, it is
one's career that must be both adventurous and exciting. It can be found
on those who plan events around the
world or set up archaeological research
sites. Traveling and
exploring will
usually be a big part
of their job, and
they may even
search for
some type
of buried
treasure—
metaphorical or
otherwise.

MOON TO EARTH: If the Icarus Line starts from the Moon Mountain and connects to the Earth Line, it means that the person has a strong need to engage in physical activities that are challenging and even experimental. These people are risk takers and thrill seekers. They may be found hang gliding, racing cars, and climbing difficult mountains.

CURVED: Sometimes, the Icarus Line curves far enough to reach the beginning edges of the Venus Mountain. These people need mental or intellectual freedom. They may be found writing or speaking out against the government, or hosting a radio talk show where they can offer views and opinions that question popular culture or typical thinking. If you have any form of the Icarus Line, you will be most happy when you throw off conformity and live an exciting and interesting life.

PART V:
CHAKRAS

✕ △ ✕

The Chakra Creases

—— ⋙ ☾ ⋘ ——

The creases etched into our palms are the chakra system of the human body. Chakras are an energy grid system, which charts the development of various material and spiritual qualities.

Chakras rarely change their courses throughout a person's life. For example, a straight and vertical Comprehension Crease will never alter its path to become a strong downward curve. Rather, an existing chakra may become deeper, lighter, shorter, or longer, or even grow a branch. However, such developments take years. Modifications like these offer evidence that energies are expanding, in use, or not used at all, depending.

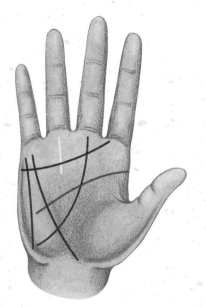

Deep or dark chakras indicate abundant potency in the fields associated with their individual meanings, while shallow or narrow creases indicate a weaker potency. Think of each crease as a flowing river. The deeper and darker the crease, the more power it carries. Like a river, a crease should also look clear and clean. If so, its energy will be substantial. However, metaphorical logs and branches—crisscrossing lines—can block the crease's path, lessening its good effects. Nicely flowing chakras show a person's strengths and capabilities, while weaker creases specify areas that need work.

Although the palm is home to many creases, each with its own significance, there are seven primary ones to look for. As you examine these creases, you'll want to pay particular attention to the shape each one takes.

Chakra Shapes

— ∧∧∧ ☾ ∨∨∨ — —

Individually examine each of the seven principal chakra creases and note their respective shapes. There are three basic forms of chakra creases on the palm: straight, curved, and wavy. The structure of the chakra reveals the spirit in which its energy is expressed.

CURVED: While one has to take into account the fact that each chakra has a different domain of influence, chakra creases that are curved will have an expression infused with subjectivity.

KEY IDEAS:
- Likes Harmony and Cooperation
- Receptive to Others
- Sees Connections
- Oriented Toward Pleasure and Enjoyment

STRAIGHT: Again bearing in mind that different chakras have different areas of influence, straight chakra creases will infuse that domain with a flavor of objectivity.

KEY IDEAS:
- Serious Minded and Self-Disciplined
- Rigid in Habits
- Objective Viewpoints/Attitudes
- Well Suited to a Business Career

WAVY: Chakras that are wavy are infused with a flavor of restlessness in their domain of influence.

KEY IDEAS:
· Difficulty Focusing
· Indecisive or Confused
· Vacillation in Work and Career
· Would Benefit from Self-Discipline

CURVED COMBINATION: Are you open when it comes to expressing your feelings? Observe your Comprehension and Emotion Chakras. If they are both curved, it is easy for you to express what is in your heart. You have a strong need to share your feelings and emotions with others.

KEY IDEAS:
- Expressive and Warmhearted
- Affectionate and Receptive
- Passionate

STRAIGHT COMBINATION: Are you closed off when it comes to expressing your feelings? Observe your Comprehension and Emotion Chakras. If they are both straight, you are self-contained. You are inclined to keep your personal feelings to yourself. Expressing your thoughts and ideas is not a problem, but you find it difficult to voice what is going on in your heart.

KEY IDEAS:
· Not Demonstrative
· Reserved and Private
· Restrained
· Passive

The Seven Chakras

— ⟶ ∿∿∿ ☾ ∿∿∿ ⟵ —

Much like the lines we've already
discussed, the Chakra Creases fall into
a set of categories—specifically, seven.
Here's a list, along with their essential
meanings or associations:

The Corporal Chakra: Sensuality

The Emotion Chakra: Love

The Comprehension Chakra:
Mental Abilities

The Communication Chakra:
Creative Expression

The Influence Chakra: Inner Strength

The Intuition Chakra: Psychic Awareness

The Security Chakra: Survival

The Corporal Chakra

— ∿∿∿ ☾ ∿∿∿ —

The personified intention of the
Corporal Chakra is "I desire."

KEY IDEAS:
- Primal Feelings
- Sexuality
  and Pleasure
- Physical
  Satisfaction
- Physical
  Desires

The Emotion Chakra

— ᜰᜰᜰ ☾ ᜰᜰᜰ — —

The personified intention of the
Emotion Chakra is "I love."

KEY IDEAS:
· Caring and
  Compassion
· Warmth
· Sharing
· Devotion
  and
  Inspiration

The Comprehension Chakra

–— ⩕⩕ ☾ ⩔⩔ —–

The personified intention of the Comprehension Chakra is "I know."

KEY IDEAS:
- Intellect and Understanding
- Concentration
- Introspection
- Thought Processing

The Communication Chakra

– – ∿∿ ☾ ∿∿ – –

The personified intention of the Communication Chakra is "I convey."

KEY IDEAS:
· Communication and Ideas
· Self-Expression
· Confidence
· Creativity

The Influence Chakra

— – ∿∿∿ ☾ ∿∿∿ – —

The personified intention of the
Influence Chakra is "I will."

KEY IDEAS:
- Inner Strength and
  Personal Power
- Determination
  and Influence
- Acceptance
  of Self
- Willpower and
  Authority

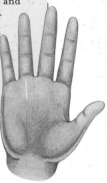

The Intuition Chakra

— ⟶ ∿∿∿ ☾ ∿∿∿ — —

The personified intention of the
Intuition Chakra is "I perceive."

KEY IDEAS:
- Insight and
  Imagination
- Extrasensory
  Awareness
- Connection
  to Other
  Dimensions
- Telepathy and
  Intuition

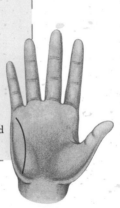

The Security Chakra

— –– ᗯᗯᗯ ☾ ᗯᗯᗯ –– —

The personified intention of the
Security Chakra is "I possess."

KEY IDEAS:
- Security and
  Stability
- The Ability to
  Achieve Goals
- Material
  Satisfaction
- Self-
  Preservation

Personality Points

— ⟶ ∿∿∿ ☾ ∿∿∿ — ⟶

There are four different personality
points. Which one you have depends
on how your Comprehension Chakra
and Corporal Chakra intersect
(or don't, as the case may be). The
different spatial relationships between
the true creases reveal your intrinsic
temperament and manner of relating
to others. Each personality point
is associated with one of the four
elements, which designates the psycho-
logical region within the universe that
you're affiliated with.

Earth Point Personality

—— ∿∿ ☾ ∿∿ ——

If your Comprehension Chakra begins below the Corporal Chakra and crosses over it, you possess an Earth Point Personality.

Those whose chakra creases begin with the Earth Point commencement strongly desire and work toward establishing solid material foundations. They are also noted for their sensible, down-to-earth thinking.

> **KEY IDEAS:**
> - Drive for Security and Stability
> - Difficulty Adapting to Change
> - Grounded, Objective Thinker
> - May Feel Insecure and Pessimistic at Times

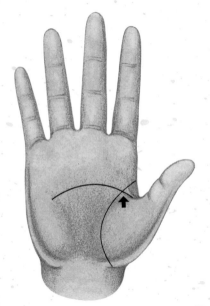

Water Point Personality

—— ⋀⋀⋀ ☾ ⋁⋁⋁ ——

If your Comprehension Chakra is
connected to the Corporal Chakra,
meaning that both creases are merged
together where they start, you possess
a Water Point Personality. This
commencement point indicates your
views and approach to life are mostly
shaped by emotional sensitivity and
family upbringing.

> **KEY IDEAS:**
> · Peaceful, Devoted, and Nurturing
> · Helpful, Gentle, and Caring
> · Possibly Self-Conscious
> · Seeks Acknowledgment and
>   Validation

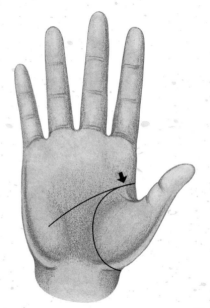

Fire Point Personality

— — ∿∿∿ ☾ ∿∿∿ — —

If your Comprehension Chakra begins significantly above the Corporal Chakra, you possess a Fire Point Personality. This indicates you highly value mental autonomy and self-reliance.

KEY IDEAS:
- Outgoing and Risk-taking
- Aggressive in Business
- Extremely Confident
- Opinionated and Bold

Air Point Personality

— ⟋⟍⟋⟍ ☾ ⟍⟋⟍⟋ —

If your Comprehension Chakra begins just above the Corporal Chakra, you are an Air Point Personality. You feel very comfortable and are most resourceful when working cooperatively with others, especially in group situations.

KEY IDEAS:
- Likes to Share and Express Opinions
- Takes Calculated Risks
- Enjoys Lively Interaction
- Conservative in Business Ventures

How to Read a Hand Quickly

— — ∿∿ ☾ ∿∿ — —

In this type of reading, we will only
use the Earth, Water, and Air Lines.
Look at these three lines, and decide
which one of the three stands out the
most. It will look the deepest and the
darkest, and it will naturally draw your
eyes. By looking at which line stands
out, you will be able to know which
basic direction a person's life will take.

EARTH: The world of physical activities is most interesting to this person. They enjoy sports and being outdoors. They will have a strong physical body. They love to build things, and may even have a career in construction. Anyone who uses their body a great deal, from athletes to farmers, will have a strong Earth Line.

WATER: This person will be very friendly and easy to be around. The world of the heart and emotions is most important to them. They are usually caring and generous. They need to have peace around them and work in a quiet area. These people like to get into activities in which they can bring out their feelings and the feelings of others.

AIR: This person will spend most of their time using their mind. They are constantly thinking, and they love collecting information and knowledge. They like to know what is going on in the world, especially the latest news and events. They may be interested in science, research, and philosophy.

About the Author

—— ᠕᠕᠕ (᠕᠕᠕ ——

Vernon Mahabal is the founder and director of the Palmistry Institute in San Francisco. In 1979, he began formal training in Vedic (Eastern) cosmology, which took him to India many times. He combines Western astrological palmistry with Chinese elemental hand analysis. He also continues new research, particularly within the field of fingerprints (dermatoglyphics). Mahabal has read thousands of hands, given hundreds of lectures, and trained hundreds of students to read palms.

Vernon hosted his own national cable show called *The Palmistry Show with Vernon Mahabal*, and has given numerous radio interviews. He has written many articles on palmistry for various periodicals, and has also been consulted by the *New York Daily News*.

The objectives of the Palmistry Institute are to further new advances in the field of hand analysis and to serve as a research and information resource. Its purpose is to restore the practice of palmistry to its rightful place as a respected and esteemed science. Vernon Mahabal can be reached at www.palmistryinstitute.com.

Acknowledgments

— — ∿∿∿ ☾ ∿∿∿ — —

Spiritual Inspirations

Srila Narayana Maharaja, Srila Satsvar-
upa Maharaja, Srila Prabhupada, Sri
Sri Radha-Govinda

Family & Friends

Mom, Syamala, Tirthapada, Jaya Sri
Clark, Jahnava Edwards, Charles
Chan, Valerie Clark & Aaron Mishkin,
Carrie, Arleen & Warren Butterworth,
Noel dela Merced, Nancy & Augustine
Reyes, Jill & Mark Koperweis, Donald
De Voe, Wendy & Ronald Smith, Alana
& Richard Unger, J. Owen Swift

Other Inspirations

William G. Betham, Ludwig van Beethoven, Black Sabbath, Trouble, Iron Maiden, Sleep, Judas Priest, Dr. Michael Savage

Extra special thanks to Jill Tabler-Koperweis for proofreading and much encouragement.

Some portions of this book were originally published in *The Secret Code on Your Hands* (2007) and *The Palmistry Deck* (2011).

MANDALA

P.O. Box 3088
San Rafael, CA 94912
www.MandalaEarth.com

CEO: Raoul Goff
President: Kate Jerome
Publisher: Roger Shaw
Associate Publisher: Mariah Bear
Editor: Ian Cannon
Editorial Assistant: Madeleine Calvi
Creative Director: Chrissy Kwasnik
Designer: Leah Lauer

ISBN 978-1-68383-931-6
Printed in China
10 9 8 7 6 5 4 3 2 1
2019 2020 2021 2022